TABLE OF CONTENTS

FOREWORD

I t is difficult to imagine that Joe Fafard's art could be made anywhere but in Saskatchewan. Whether the artist is modelling the rural image of the cow to which he is almost obsessively attached, or rendering evocative likenesses of artistic friends, both present and past, Fafard's work is a product of his personal history and his lifetime commitment to his prairie home.

It is therefore our special tribute to Joe Fafard, a senior Saskatchewan artist who has contributed a great deal to our own sense of place, that *Joe Fafard: Cows and Other Luminaries 1977-1987* is presented jointly by the Mendel Art Gallery, Saskatoon, and the Dunlop Art Gallery, Regina. We take this opportunity to extend a public handshake to each other, for this has been a collaboration of common dedication.

But the opportunity of working on this important project was made possible first and foremost by the artist, Joe Fafard. We are grateful for the intensity of his commitment, the playfulness of his humor, and the keenness of his vision.

The exhibition catalogue is comprised of four texts, an in-depth interview with the artist and biographical notes. These have been contributed by Matthew Teitelbaum, Curator, Mendel Art Gallery, and Peter White, Regina.

The contributions of the lenders to *Joe Fafard: Cows and Other Luminaries 1977-1987* cannot be overestimated. Without their generosity and their sense of community pride, this exhibition would not have been possible.

All of us welcome Northern Telecom Canada Limited as the sponsor of this exhibition. It has been a pleasure to join with them in the presentation of a major artistic voice in Saskatchewan.

Linda Milrod
Director
Mendel Art Gallery
Saskatoon

Peter White
Curator/Director
Dunlop Art Gallery
Regina

The support of The Canada Council and the Saskatchewan Arts Board is acknowledged here with gratitude.

JOE FAFARD

COWS AND OTHER LUMINARIES 1977-1987

MATTHEW TEITELBAUM
PETER WHITE

MENDEL ART GALLERY, SASKATOON
DUNLOP ART GALLERY, REGINA

This exhibition has been made possible with a grant from
Northern Telecom Canada Limited.

Mendel Art Gallery, Saskatoon, 2 October to 15 November 1987

Dunlop Art Gallery, Regina, 12 December 1987 to 17 January 1988

Published for the exhibition *Joe Fafard: Cows and Other Luminaries 1977-1987* by
the Mendel Art Gallery and the Dunlop Art Gallery, nonprofit organizations
supported by City of Saskatoon, the Regina Public Library Board, Province of
Saskatchewan, Saskatchewan Arts Board, The Canada Council, and Museum
Assistance Programmes of the National Museums of Canada.

Photography: All photographs are by Grant Kernan, Saskatoon, with the following
exceptions: figs. 1 and 4, Espace 5, Montreal; fig. 2, Norman Mackenzie Art Gallery;
figs. 3 and 5, Eberhard Otto; fig. 6, Courtesy of the Toronto-Dominion Centre,
Daniel Weiner; fig. 8, George Moppett.

Designer: McKay Goettler and Associates, Saskatoon

Printer: Houghton Boston, Saskatoon

Mendel Art Gallery, 950 Spadina Crescent East, P.O. Box 569, Saskatoon,
Saskatchewan, Canada, S7K 3L6, (306) 975-7610

Dunlop Art Gallery, Regina Public Library, 2311-12th Avenue, P.O. Box 2311,
Regina, Saskatchewan, Canada, S4P 3Z5, (306) 569-7576

©Mendel Art Gallery and Dunlop Art Gallery 1987

ISBN: 0-919863-36-1

Cover: 35. *Vincent* (1985)
Bronze, patina and oil paint (2/7)
99.7 × 68.5 × 19.2 cm
Courtesy of the artist and Susan Whitney Gallery, Regina

ACKNOWLEDGMENTS

31. *Vic* (1984)
Clay, glaze and acrylic paint

Throughout the course of organizing this exhibition, we have benefitted from the advice and cooperation of many individuals. We wish to thank Susan Whitney of Susan Whitney Gallery, Regina, and Doug Udell and Roger Woltjen of Woltjen/Udell Gallery, Edmonton. They helped locate important works for this exhibition and assisted in numerous other ways. Pat James, curator of the Toronto-Dominion Bank Collection, Toronto, kindly provided photographs of *The Pasture* for reproduction.

Our very special thanks are extended to all lenders to this exhibition. They not only graciously invited us into their homes and offices, but their willingness to lend their works has helped to make this exhibition what we hoped it might be.

The staffs of our respective institutions played an important role in the assembly and realization of the exhibition. It is with pleasure that we acknowledge the contributions of Virginia Ebbels, Leona Kindrachuk, Helen Marzolf, Suzanne Probe and Jack Severson of the Dunlop Art Gallery, and Gary Boehm, Bonnie Gerwing, Judy Koutecky, Perry Opheim, Susan Sarich, Sylvia Tritthardt and Coleen Wilson of the Mendel Art Gallery.

Finally, our warm thanks are extended to Susan and Joe Fafard, who have involved themselves in many ways in the preparation of this exhibition. Susan located important documentary sources for our consideration and read our texts in draft form with much appreciated care. Joe has talked generously about various aspects of his career and has responded openly and encouragingly to our numerous conjectures about his work. We have learned a great deal from each of them.

Matthew Teitelbaum
Peter White

8. *Calf* (1980)
Clay and glaze

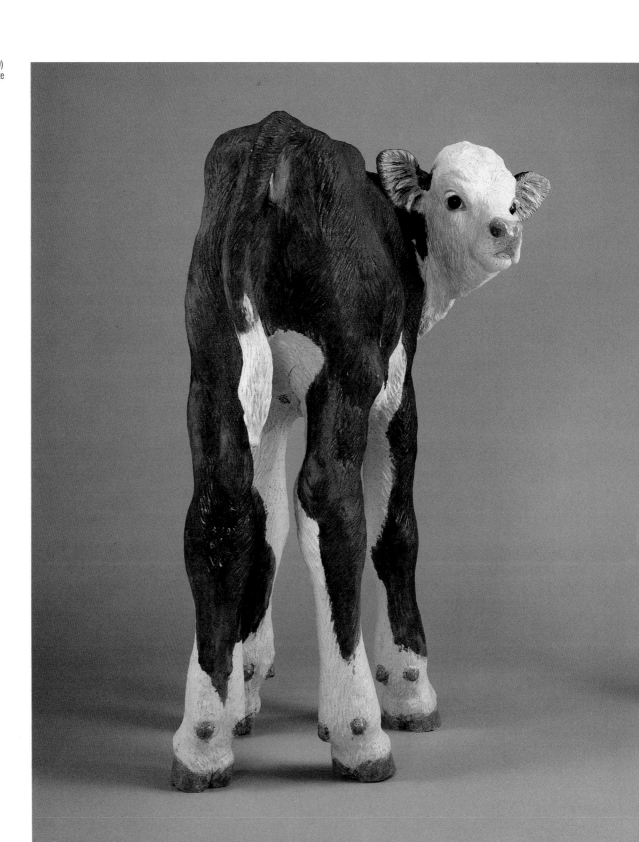

INTRODUCTION

J oe Fafard: Cows and Other Luminaries 1977-1987 takes as its point of departure The Edmonton Art Gallery's 1979 travelling exhibition *Joe Fafard*. Much of Fafard's reputation and acclaim has been based on the popular clay genre figures featured in that show. Since that time, Fafard has continued to focus on the familiar cow and portraits of friends and artistic luminaries. With these two subject types, his work raises important issues about place, community, humor, tradition and artistic persona. His intense preoccupation with these subjects has been underlined through his use of a widening variety of formats and media.

Fafard has created his art out of the cherished experiences of small-town Saskatchewan and his work, as much as anything, is inspired by his own heartfelt allegiances and friendships. It reflects, in part, his own intense desire to stake a claim in the territory of art. Fafard has continually attacked the authority which art critics and other outsiders would seem to have held over the Saskatchewan art community. His rejection of the outsider's dominance runs parallel with a strong belief that important and lasting value can be created from a lifetime of experience within a community. Recalling his participation at the 1968 Emma Lake Artists' Workshop, for example, Fafard declared a belief that all artists should "make art out of our own experiences . . . [art] should be coming straight out of life."[1] His declaration was, in fact, quite clear: ". . . we should abolish the reverence that we have for outsiders [and authority]."[2] Fafard's sense of community has been created from a feeling of social coherence, shared expectation and common ritual. It is the touchstones of this community – cooperation, a developed work ethic, loyalty and personal fortitude – which bind his subjects.

Fafard's definition of community is not limited by specific time or place. It is rooted in both experience and the imagination. His own sense of personal experience encompasses real and present events as well as fanciful projections onto personalities from history books. Memory, family history and an open-eyed admiration have led Fafard to expand his subject matter beyond the everyday and the familiar to a wider kinship. He began through portraits of historical figures from his regional community; in recent years he has looked at art history for a new branch of ancestors. In doing so, he has surrounded himself with a kind of home-grown inspiration: portraits of artists he deeply admires but never knew. By defining community as a state of mind, Fafard has created representations from his celebratory imagination.

1. John King, *"A Documented Study of the Artists' Workshop at Emma Lake, Saskatchewan, from 1955 to 1970"* (BFA thesis, University of Manitoba, 1971), 193.
2. King, 319.

(fig. 1) *Cree Man* (1975)
Clay and glaze
44.5 × 37.0 × 30.0 cm

t lies at the center of the creative life: the moment of doubt. For Fafard, in the summer and early fall of 1969, this moment stretched into a sustained questioning of his trained sensibility as a "modernist" artist. As a sessional lecturer at the University of Saskatchewan, Regina, Fafard had begun to teach on the foundations of his own training. He had graduated from the masters of fine arts program at Pennsylvania State University in 1968 and had returned to Saskatchewan with a sculptural vocabulary filled with grand gestures, a hint of comic absurdity, and, perhaps most telling of all, a skeptical take on the sacredness of the scale and finish of natural form. His work, mostly student work to that point, included an oversized child's high-chair, mammoth french fries made of foam rubber (à la pop guru, Claes Oldenberg), and a motorized rotating seven-foot tall tree caught in a never-ending frenzied hoola-hoop dance (fig. 2). His objects, exquisitely crafted and with all their art world references, took quick jabs at an overly verbalized art world. Not work of sensibility, this was work of an intelligent, critical cynicism. It was hip. It was part of a generalized critique of a new technological and commercial age, and it referred to the New York Pop artists of the early 1960s. This engagement led to Fafard's doubt, a doubt that began with a questioning of sources and influences which were removed from his personal experience in rural Saskatchewan. Such questioning was seen, at least retrospectively, as a conflict between environments – the metropolis and the rural community. "For me," Fafard was quoted in 1975, "it's important that I have a link with the countryside because I'm a country person; my life was shaped by the country."[1]

Fafard's burning desire in the late 1960s, although not an articulated one, was to find his own place in Saskatchewan's contemporary art scene. Here the push towards formalist abstraction had for some time held sway. Guided by the presence and critical writings of American critic Clement Greenberg, many Saskatchewan artists – the Regina Five, William Perehudoff and Otto Rogers among them – worked through a process of artmaking that was rigorous in principle, rooted in aesthetic judgment and decidedly international in outlook. For Fafard, the search for place within the place he called his own was determined by his reaction to the polished, slippery surface of the formalist position. All things said in defense of the formalist canon came to represent, for Fafard, the very issues he was driven to rebel against. Where the formalist position asserted that a work of art should not describe a lived experience, but rather should set up an abstract equivalent for it, Fafard's question was: why *only* that? When the formalist position asserted that a work of art should be devoid of literary reference or a literal understanding of experience, Fafard also asked why.

(fig. 2) *Synthetic Tree* (1968)
Expanded plastic and motor
192 cm (height)

What Fafard feared – no, resented – was a sense that judgments about works of art could be made without regard for the particular, the intimate or the personal. He questioned judgments which could be made only on the basis of theoretical or universal principles; he questioned the outsider's authority. In 1970, reflecting on his experience at the 1968 Emma Lake Workshop led by Donald Judd, Fafard noted:

> As an experience I really thought it was great to have. Anyway, I didn't have any regrets about it because, personally, I really didn't feel the need to go there and listen to some big guy from New York give me the lowdown on what's what . . . I was going there and dealing with other people and not going there to be sort of purified by the leader.[2]

Fafard's doubt intensified at this point: where dissatisfaction with his own work met the stifling predictability of the formalist alternatives proposed in his own art community. The issue for Fafard was the power of the dominant art centers to establish appropriateness, or proper ambition, for artists working elsewhere.

At the beginning of the fall term in 1969, the California artist David Gilhooly joined the faculty of the university's visual arts department. For Fafard, Gilhooly's move to Regina offered a new set of possibilities. He brought with him his own distrust of art world authority and an apprenticeship with a generation of California sculptors who were looking for, and finding, "something of their own which they could do in the most versatile of all mediums, clay of course."[3] Gilhooly's manner of working, and the sculptures he realized, came out of a loosely defined Funk sensibility. They were irreverent, ironic, and satirical: frogs frying in butter and mythic creatures balancing radishes on the tips of their noses. It was an embracing attitude which called back to the Dada artists of the 1920s for company, sharing an indifference to exquisite, elegant or well-balanced form, and a desire to challenge anyone who wanted to assert a definition of art. In the fullest manifestation of their art, Funk sculptors looted the junk piles to make assemblages of various kinds. Gilhooly juxtaposed representations of unlikely forms but did so in single, discrete ceramic objects; the image was visually chaotic, yet the material was consistent, unified and contained the evidence of the artist's craft.

Gilhooly's crazy and unexpected contrasts of objects – whether real or represented – suggested a basic challenge to the sacred edge of the modernist tradition. References to the familiar, domestic world were abundant and, as twisted as they were to the level of absurdity, they commented on the relationship of art to everyday life. Just what that was, Fafard had begun to explore in his own work in the autumn of 1969, a few months after Gilhooly's arrival.[4] Gilhooly's example pulled from Fafard's past his own playful engagement with plaster and clay. While an undergraduate at the University of Manitoba, Fafard had

(fig. 3) *Michael Haynee, 107 years old* (1971) Clay, glaze and acrylic paint 37.1 × 19.1 × 27.8 cm

worked plaster into large-scale, free-standing figures, full of descriptive detail. During his master's program at Penn State, he had taken real pleasure in working in the pottery workshop. When a number of his kinetic wood and metal pieces were shown in a group exhibition in his last year, he chose to include free standing plaster figures again – not as works in the exhibition – but as spectators, added to the crowd, inanimate but always there. Fafard repressed whatever affection he had for those figures in favor of what he then considered loftier ideals of serious material and subject. In 1969, the California example knocked Fafard's faith to the ground. It pointed to alternative sources in his own experience: experiences which were familiar and affectionately remembered.

In the autumn of 1969, a new series of plaster works emerged from an isolated campus studio. When they were first shown in the corridors of the university's department of visual arts, those who passed by were taken by surprise. These were life-sized plaster busts of Fafard's department colleagues, crudely realized and roughly painted. They contained the excitement of a reintroduction to familiar material. The clumsiness of their handling related them to a tradition of cartoon caricature.

More ceramic figures quickly followed – again members of the visual arts faculty and art world types – taken to a further, satirical edge. With a biting, though not contradictory, mixture of affection and ridicule, Fafard sent up the stylistic trappings of all institutional art worlds. He portrayed an art historian, known for his penchant for contemporary fashion, as a clothes horse with four sturdy hooves, while the curator of the university gallery, enveloped in a color-field cape, assumed whatever ridiculed authority he could through the giant rubbery pencil which grew from his elbow.

The "rogues gallery" of plaster figures, and the ceramic figures which followed, focused Fafard's disillusionment and led him to define his own values in the making of physical objects. In probing everyday experience for subject matter, he began to discover a position for himself. He did so by accepting blatantly referential subject matter as the stuff of his art. Then, most encouragingly, he turned to a cherished world of positive values. The clay medium, with its associations of everyday craft and the domestic, led away from satire. His subsequent portraits were deferential, affectionate character studies, homages to a past life and time. His first subject was the 107-year-old father of a department janitor. In 1975, Fafard recalled the genesis of *Michael Haynee, 107 years old* (1971) (fig. 3):

> I met this man and we had tea, and somehow you just can't treat a person who is [107] years old in a very light way – you have to be quite serious about it! So I made this fairly accurate portrait of the old man, sitting like an Egyptian on a chair, very stalwart and very solid. And I reflected on all the things that this man must've gone through in his life, you know, being born in 1863 . . . [being alive and around in 1971.][5]

11

(fig. 4) *George #2* (1974)
Clay, glaze and acrylic paint
40.5 × 22.5 × 31.0 cm

The values of a lifetime, the importance of history and place, the humility of private experience: all tied Fafard to new subject matter. At issue was the particularity of a personality. Whatever generalized values could be pulled from his portrait of Alley Haynee's father, they were rooted in Fafard's understanding of how personality was formed by experience.

Inherent in Fafard's work was a sense of community. In late 1971 he settled in the small town of Pense, twenty miles west of Regina.[6] In his new community he found his subject matter all around him. Without any desire for comprehensiveness, Fafard began to portray the people of Pense: Hank, King, Geoffrey, Al, Eva, George (fig. 4). These were chronicles of a life, and they were rooted in direct observation. Consideration of personal habit turned slowly to a picture show of community values or customs. The particular slouch, the frayed workman's collar, the well-worn shoes – all combined, in portrait after portrait, to suggest a real and breathing social coherence.

It was, in fact, Fafard's idealized world, rock solid on the foundation of humanist values. An essentially romantic desire led him to highlight virtue in the evidence of hard work and personal self-assurance. He worked hard to underline these values in his portrait chronicles. Fafard saw that work rooted these people to their place, a place of comfortable familiarity and social ease, however far away from a dominating center they were. Significantly, his work rooted him and his family within the community. For Fafard:

> You just live as if it's life. I just carry out my work, and I seek out the experiences of the life of the community the same way as anybody else in the community does. I participate in the bingo or a whist drive if I have the time, you know, and go curling or to the hockey-games.[7]

M.T.

1. Geoffrey Ursell, "Fafard," *Emerging Arts West* (October 1975): 33.

2. John King, *"A Documented Study of the Artists' Workshop at Emma Lake, Saskatchewan, from 1955 to 1970"* (BFA thesis, University of Manitoba, 1971), 193.

3. David Gilhooly, "Introduction: As Gilhooly Remembers It," in *The Continental Clay Connection*, ed. Maija Bismanis (Regina: Norman Mackenzie Art Gallery, 1980), 4.

4. Fafard had been amused and tantalized by ceramic work before. In the winter of 1969 the exhibition, *California Ceramics*, was mounted at the Norman Mackenzie Art Gallery. Of particular importance were Richard Shaw's comical figures. They sat among the rounded cushions of loveseats without expression. Everything about them – their bright clothing, their sturdy posture – signalled their lives in mid-America.

5. Ursell, 33.

6. He did not leave the university until his resignation in February of 1974.

7. Ursell, 31.

12

(fig. 5) *Mon Père* (1972)
Earthenware, acrylic glaze
34.1 × 35.4 × 35.4 cm

9. *Ceramic Bull* (1980)
Clay, glaze and acrylic paint

From the time that he began to draw upon his own life and environment for subject matter and inspiration, a constant of Joe Fafard's art has been cattle: cows, bulls, calves. He admits to being addicted to making them and, despite attempts to quit, says all this has ever done is make him uptight. Fafard has related this compulsion to artistic process. Making this animal is a form of exercise that keeps the basics limber, and, somewhat paradoxically, the imagination in shape. Unlike human portraiture, where peculiarities of individual personality and situation must be addressed, Fafard approaches the cow as an inherently neutral and abstract form with which he feels he can be almost automatically free and experimental in the examination of formal concerns: mass, weight, scale, proportion, volume, surface, color, etc. Fafard has made hundreds upon hundreds of cows. He has made them for the pedestal, in miniature and larger than life-size. He has made them with a verisimilitude that is stunning but has also twisted and pulled them into a wide range of shapes and attitudes. He has made them individually, in series, in tableaux, and in materials that include clay, papier-mâché and, more recently, bronze. Cows have also been the subject of many prints and paintings.

Despite his preoccupation with this motif, the cow has been virtually ignored in the critical discussion of Fafard's art, as if it somehow represented a failure of real creative imagination. This is perhaps not surprising given that Fafard has consistently emphasized its role in connection with formal and technical concerns. Yet, notwithstanding the essential place of formal investigation and discovery in his art, which is directly relatable to the remarkable physical quality of his sculpture and its often majestic esthetic presence, it is difficult to imagine how such fascination and freshness of vision could be sustained through the production of so many of these creatures, over a period of more than fifteen years, without a more complex and personal attachment and meaning.

Certainly there is no arbitrariness in the choice of this subject. Fafard's familiarity with the cow goes back to childhood. When he was growing up on a family farm in Ste. Marthe, Saskatchewan, near the Manitoba border, cows were a fixture of his life. As Fafard has suggested: if this animal provided a means of support through its milk, cheese, butter, meat and hide, it also extracted a high price in the time and effort, little of it pleasant, that went into caring for its considerable needs. ''I have spent much of my life working for cows,'' Fafard has said not altogether facetiously. "After a while you don't know who is using whom."[1] He also adds that, when it comes down to it, to a certain extent our own bodies are composed of "cow material." Doubtless such symbiosis and upsetting of the evolutionary equation add a distancing note of bemused absurdity to his interest in the cow. Yet it is also clear that however much he is attracted to it as a form, the cow represents something integral to his life and outlook. "For me it's so natural I can't think about it. It's like fish can't think about wet." Such ties, then, have a personal imprimatur, a bond lacking in the intellectually imposed, impersonal and experientially hidebound art theories he rejected. Whatever else the cow might suggest, it has an intrinsic significance as a constant reminder of who he is, a point of contact both with the most elementary aspects of his life and what he believes must be their central place in his art. Not only might this explain why Fafard has always entrusted formal experimentation to the cow, but it also relates to the question of imagination. For what is at issue here is not necessarily originality or profound insight but continuity. Repeated continuously, Fafard's cow is a means of connecting reason with experience, of representing himself to himself as well as to others.[2]

Ordinarily the cow is not thought of in heroic terms. It is not an animal that has occasioned the romantic worship that has been heaped in modern times, for example, upon the horse. Nonetheless, as a symbol of stable, indomitable steadfastness and reliability, the domestic cow takes on its own kind of heroism in Fafard's art. It takes its meaning in the context of a valued rural, regional existence that may not have tamed but has come to terms with the vagaries of climate and external economic forces and the resistance of the land itself. Although it is not linked, like images of cows in seventeenth-century Dutch art, to prosperity, it can be seen to share with these precursors the expression of a pastoral ideal strongly tempered, but nonetheless enriched, by reality. Rather than a prop of arcadian fantasy or bucolic idyll, the cow here is the living symbol of pragmatism, of human perseverance and domestic self-reliance. The feelings encompassed by such an ideal are basic ones – well-being, psychological security, peacefulness, harmony with nature – all understood in the context of a keenly felt sense of time, place and community. Moreover, underlying Fafard's cows is an assertion of pride in and identification with a society that, despite the indifference or self-interest, as the case may be, of the outside world, knows and accepts itself on what are its own, predominantly egalitarian, terms. In this sense the common cow becomes an emblem of both virtue and defiance.

6. *Bull* (1979)
Clay, glaze and acrylic paint

To read such meaning into Fafard's cows may raise questions even as it attempts to answer them. Yet the significance of this animal would seem apparent from the idealized terms of its expression, which is as the object of a framework or structure, mythic in nature, for the memory and attitudes of the past, in particular those of childhood. Fafard: ''The cow keeps me in touch with the kid inside me. Adults don't have the same innocent observation I had on the farm.'' The cow is the link to childhood and its perspective which, as the poet and critic Eli Mandel has so forcefully argued in his writings on prairie literature, is at the heart of the meaning of regionalism:

> . . . from the adult's point of view, the child's vision is a vision of innocence, of a lost Eden; another way of putting this is that the child's vision – again from the adult's point of view – is of home; and that surely is the essence of what we mean by a region, the overpowering feeling of nostalgia associated with the place we know as the *first* place, the *first* vision of things, the *first* clarity of things.[3]

Mandel's understanding of the prairie as a myth of childhood has been contested, among other reasons, because it lacks environmental specificity.[4] But, as Mandel contends, a view that confines itself to environmental factors is inevitably literal and realist. Such expression, he believes, is ''essentially superficial,'' given to cliché and stereotype. In contrast, the notion of the prairie as ''mental construct, a region of the mind, a myth,'' subsumes the impact of the landscape within a broader vision that adapts ''images of the environment to a pattern that belongs to all men.'' It is not, then, the facts themselves that generate a sense of region but, transformed by memory as myth, it is the impression these particulars make and the role they play as a site for the framing and comprehension of one's experience and place in the world. As understood here, regionalism connotes an attitude or point of view in which the region is vision's emotional center of gravity but is by no means its limit.

Made in relation to the point of view of the child, Fafard's cows might be seen as marvels of mythic dimension and weight. The language is not realist but, as Mandel suggests, has two aspects. One is a kind of magic realism, an enhanced form ''objective and dream-like.'' This heightened or magic quality is especially pronounced in a number of cows Fafard made in the late 1970s. The white *Baby Bull* (1977) (cat. 1), for example, seems to distill innocence and purity. As well, given this mythicized context, it has a sweetness that reads not as sentimental excess but the warmth of deep feeling. Other works from this time, such as *Ceramic Bull* (1980) (cat. 9), are fantastic and almost

1. *Baby Bull* (1977)
Clay, glaze and acrylic paint

unreal in their combination of the exaggerated impression of solidity and mass with a highly sensuous smoothness of body texture. While such qualities mark an apogee to date in Fafard's technical control and handling of clay, they are also what make these works among his most demonstrative and arresting depictions, emotionally and conceptually, of these animals. More recently, through the move to casting in bronze, Fafard has utilized that medium for related effect. The bronze cows in *The Pasture* (fig. 6), the outdoor installation Fafard created for the Toronto-Dominion Centre in downtown Toronto in 1985, are not only literally weighty but their impact is magnified and their familiarity transformed by their repetition – the same cow seven times – impressive size – one-seventh larger than the actual size of an average cow – and the rich, steadily deepening patina of their surfaces.

The other voice through which region is expressed is the region's own vernacular language. Notwithstanding his formative connections to West Coast Funk, itself strongly informed by popular art forms and media, Fafard's work relates strongly to the popular culture of prairie society. Just how much is evident in the ease with which Fafard's own cows could be seen to mingle with popular images. In one of the many mass media articles that appeared in the seventies on Fafard and his small-town life in Pense, Suzanne Zwarun wrote:

> The big, rambling house with the splayed veranda and the hops growing into the third story studio window is crammed with hundreds of cows in various stages of creation. It's a dizzying assortment of Fafard's own cows, kitsch and china cows sent by friends, antique cows unearthed by admirers. Cow decals decorate the windows and walls, the refrigerator and the van he drives. Cows are painted on glass and canvas, cow tiles line a sink, a black, clay cows' hoof lies discarded on a drainboard. Cows march across shelves, over mantelpieces, up windowsills and a life-size calf leans in a corner, a joint project of Fafard and his mother. Cows decorate the peepholes in his kiln and march across his shirts.[5]

In this vernacular, correctness of form and accuracy of detail are not an issue. Mandel suggests oral tradition, prose rather than poetry, tall tales and the like as the characteristic forms of this expression in which accessibility and the ability to communicate vividly take precedence over style or art. Aspects of all this are clearly evident in Fafard's cows. Going back to his early days in Pense, his cows were notable for their loosely handled forms, their apparent lack of refinement and punchy glazes. Throughout this decade, his cows have come out in a variety of exaggerated and fancifully distorted shapes and sizes. The effect is humorous, playful, friendly. But, like the tall tale, it is not at all un-serious in its capacity to draw fascinated attention to the experience

11. *Daisy I* (1980)
Clay and glaze

33. *Untitled* (1985)
Bronze and patina (1/7)

and commitment out of which it comes. A significant connection exists with folk art. This includes Fafard's own mother's folk art, which included the making of papier-mâché cows and, most importantly for him, constituted an "ethics of making things." Although the essential patterns of Fafard's art making were in place by the time he became fully aware of folk art in the mid-1970s, he felt great affinity with the humor, directness and connection to place of these artists whose aspirations and standards were high, although not necessarily consonant with those of high art. Discussing his interest in folk artists, Fafard wrote in 1979:

> I admire untutored artists as much as tutored ones. Why not? Why should one make a distinction? All artists create from the same impulse which expresses itself to the artist in the form of a need, like eating, or passing wind.[6]

At the heart of the regionalist impulse is the question of origins. In *The Pasture*, Fafard transposed his to invest that urban, commercial site with its own rural beginnings. Modern, contemporary life, bustling and focused upon itself, is confronted and forced into dialogue with a history seemingly spurned by, in this instance, Mies van der Rohe's abstractly elegant, densely clustered steel and glass structures. If Fafard's cows, spread out in self-absorbed repose on their carpet of grass, proffer pastoral calm in the midst of these glittering towers, their tone is also provocative in their articulation of clear, succinct divisions – urban-rural, center-region, present-past, culture-nature. *The Pasture* may not shift the balance or, in any real sense, heal such rifts. However, as a constant presence, it invokes the humility implied by the recognition of a past that is not only shared with others but on which the urban region continues, practically and otherwise, to so heavily depend.

P.W.

1. Comments by the artist are from conversations with the author June 9 and June 11, 1987.

2. See Edward Said, "On Repetition," *The World, the Text and the Critic* (Cambridge: Harvard University Press, 1983), 113.

3. Eli Mandel, "Images of Prairie Man," in *A Region of the Mind: Interpreting the Western Canadian Plains*, ed. Richard Allen (Regina: Canadian Plains Studies Centre, 1973), 206.

4. See E.A. McCourt, "Prairie Literature and Its Critics," in *A Region of the Mind: Interpreting the Western Canadian Plains*, ed. Richard Allen (Regina: Canadian Plains Studies Centre, 1973), 153-164.

5. Suzanne Zwarun, "That Artist Fella," *Maclean's*, vol. 90, no. 15 (1977), 24.

6. Joe Fafard in Eli Mandel, ed., "A Comprehensible World," *artscanada* 36 (October/November 1979): 19.

(fig. 6) *The Pasture* (1985)
Bronze and patina
Seven cows, each 106.7 × 274.3 × 152.4 cm

16. *My Art Critic* (1980)
Clay and acrylic paint

A caricature of a face admits that its owner has had a past, but denies that he has a future. He has arrested his features up to a certain point, but now they have taken charge of him so that he can never change; he has become a single possibility completely realized.[1]

Viewed head on, it reads as an oversized but otherwise conventional portrait bust. Viewed in profile, it is radically, comically compressed, depicting the man in terms of the attribute that is understood to stand for his entire thought and point of view. It may be doing Clement Greenberg an injustice to reduce his critical theory to the issue of flatness, yet it is difficult to imagine a gesture that could cut to the heart of the matter more incisively or more fittingly than the send up realized by this blunt, but in its own way, most elegant visual pun.

My Art Critic (cat. 16), one of four Greenberg portraits Joe Fafard made in 1980, may seem to have lacked timeliness. By 1980, reaction to Greenberg's formalism, its arbitrariness and its exclusions, was widespread. His ontology, with its view of painting progressing by degrees to a state in which image, expunged of spatial illusion, became congruent with the flat surface of the physical support, not only had lost its persuasiveness but, upon reflection, could be seen to be based on an eccentrically subjective misreading of modern art. Even in western Canada, where Greenberg's influence still had strength, inspiring work that most often applied his ideas in a kind of dry, programmatic, after-the-fact way, his dominance was an issue that had been more or less settled. Fafard's earlier determined efforts to deal with his own experience and what was personally meaningful, at a time when Greenberg was not only a force generally but, through his personal presence in the West, a local one there as well, had had something to do with this. Nonetheless, there was a convincing sense of necessity in the Greenberg portraits. However disparaged, Greenberg's ideas had then, as they do now, a remarkable resilience. As Kay Larson has pointed out in an appraisal of the Greenberg phenomenon, to this day they continue to exert a "subliminal inhibiting force" in constituting a point of view around which artists, consciously or otherwise, position themselves.[2] Further, again as Larson notes, Greenberg's ideas cannot be separated from a dictatorial personal disposition, "the perverse magnetism of the authoritarian personality, the charm of contemptuousness."[3] Fafard had not only personally experienced this aspect of Greenberg, but, as an artist in Regina who had rejected his ideas, he was subject to the emotions and pressures Greenberg was capable of stirring. To Fafard, Greenberg was a flash point for the alienating tensions and divisions within his own community, an "anti-Christ" whose message, made without compromise, was that community is irrelevant to art.[4]

Fafard is not easy on Greenberg in these portraits. In the case of *My Art Critic*, there is more than a little malice in turning Greenberg's own concepts upon themselves and him, making flatness read as shallowness or narrowness. With the discrepancy between its frontal view and profile, the piece also suggests that, contrary to Greenberg's absolutism, appearances not only are deceptive but that how one sees things depends on one's point of view. Moreover, the format of the portrait bust objectifies the subject who, disembodied as idea, can be seen as the inevitably freakish realization of his own skewed logic. Fafard took other pokes at Greenberg. If the size of *My Art Critic* refers to him in terms of ego, the miniature *Model of Clem* (1980) (cat. 15) literally cuts him down to size, the disdain compounded by the fact Fafard did not take the trouble to finish painting in the back of the figure. *Bust of Clem* (1980) (cat. 7) is not flattened. It is monochromatic. The effect is visually interesting yet one that demonstrates a clear lack of commitment to its subject by denying it the benefit of a full representation. In the standing figure *Clem* (1980) (cat. 10), Greenberg appears dapper; the pose he strikes is one of apparent confidence. Yet the projected image does not hold up. It is evident, for example, that the jacket, creeping up at the back, is a wornout, shrunken remnant of what it might once have been and that the pose itself is misleading, betrayed by a slight stoop and a facial expression that carries more than a hint of bemused vacancy.

Without doubt, Fafard makes his point. Yet Greenberg does not come across simply as a grotesque. Rather, with a degree of charity not always shared by Greenberg himself, whose own modernist-centered values involved a particularly healthy contempt for those he saw as "provincial,"[5] these works evoke considerable pathos. They depict decline, linking Greenberg's personal and physical reality – he was by this time well past his prime – with the fortunes of his fading reputation and stature. In this sense, Greenberg's shabby clothes, his pose and expression are signs of a sad but human reality. Contrasted to his own understanding of art as a system of objects and objective formal values, Greenberg is presented as a person in these pieces. As such they constitute an altogether successful assertion of Fafard's own point of view and position.

10. *Clem* (1980)
Clay, glaze and acrylic paint

2. *Bird* (1977)
Screenprint

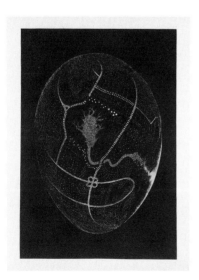

5. *DC-Neuf* (1978)
Screenprint

In terms of the direction Fafard's art was to take, the Greenberg portraits now appear pivotal. Although he did not, in any sense, feel a lack of interest in the pursuit of interests centered on his life in Pense and his rural Saskatchewan background, Fafard was anxious to examine new possibilities. When the idea of Greenberg presented itself, it made sense as a vehicle for reflection and definition.[6] In their very choice of subjects, Fafard's Pense portraits had always involved a strong critical stance, one in which the high art values identified with Greenberg were notable if only for being so blatantly disregarded. In the Greenberg portraits, however, this critical substructure is made explicit. Moreover, it is given great immediacy in that it is spelled out in terms of the imposing and controversial figure of Greenberg himself. While not necessarily dismissive of criticism as such, these works confront the critical mentality that is inherently elitist, intellectual rather than social or moral in its biases, and prescriptive in its expression. Here the use of clay, with its craft associations, willful representation as opposed to abstract imagery, and lack of formal elegance is itself an explicit statement of artistic identity and belief. The key, however, is Fafard's humor, in particular the visual punning, writ large, of *My Art Critic*. The pun is a form Greenberg would hate. Whereas his own approach is that of a refined, formal sensibility, buttressed by a sense of history and mission, the pun is primitive, spontaneous, playful, anarchistic. Moreover, not only is it humorous but it is virtually the lowest kind of humor.

Humor can be human and liberating; it can be a critical weapon. The pun itself is transgressive; it is about possibility, breaking or flying in the face of established rules of order and decorum. In his study of the pun, Walter Redfern notes the pun is about ''undoing certainties, making them come apart at the 'semes'.''[7] Yet it also has, in contrast to high art, a populist aspect. It is a ''democratic trope,'' a ''free-for-all available to everyone.''[8] If the pun functions as a form of criticism, in a broader sense it is ''a whole way of feeling, seeing, thinking and expressing.''[9] In relation to Fafard, what began as an affront to Greenberg and all he represents evolved as a means of projecting and alluding to the very values and critical assumptions upon which the conduct of his life and art are predicated. This may explain why he has persisted in flattening long after *My Art Critic*. However removed from the primary critical issues that generated it, for Fafard, flattening carries meaningful, vestigial reference.

  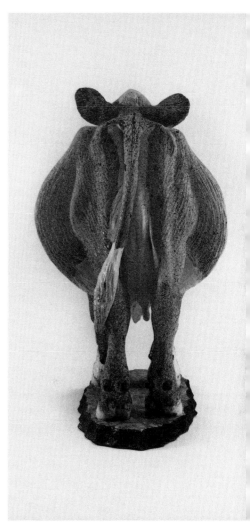

21. *Cow in Space Wrinkle* (1982)
Clay and glaze

22. *House Bull*
23. *Pet Cow*
(side view)

Fafard's interest in the critical and humorous potential of flatness, illusion and visual point of view predates the Greenberg portraits. In two screenprints he made in the late seventies, *Bird* (1977) (cat. 2) and *DC-Neuf* (1978) (cat. 5), an overhead or bird's-eye-view is utilized. While some depth or relief is suggested in *Bird*, the lengthening shadows of the cows and fence posts, together with a continuous green, framing apron, force the issue of the material flatness of the picture plane. In *DC-Neuf*, on the other hand, the world, when viewed from above, appears round or, rather, oval. The joke is partly that the earth, criss-crossed by patterns formed by bands of brightly lit roadways, bears a resemblance to the highly decorated Easter eggs of the region's large Ukrainian population. However, in terms of spatial illusion, the humor of the print is its play on the misguided conviction of those who, convinced by the arrogance of personal logic, once stubbornly held to the notion that the world was flat. This question arose again several years later when Fafard, while preparing to teach a semester at the University of California at Davis, became intrigued by an implication of E.H. Gombrich's famous book, *Art and Illusion*. While the book's title referred to art, it was evident that what it really was about was illusion in painting. Responding to what he perceived as the privileged position of painting as an issue for sculpture, Fafard began to experiment with foreshortening his cows. These form the immediate background to *My Art Critic*. A number of years later, in 1983, Fafard approached the problem in a different way, making landscape, a genre associated with painting, accessible to sculpture in a series of three-dimensional ''lampscapes,'' the spatial illusion of which was in some cases extended to infinity by the use of mirrors. More generally, the bias toward painting, so strongly reflected in Greenberg's thought, became firmly embedded within the larger critical context in which Fafard has continued to co-opt flatness for his own purposes in sculpture.

Fafard's use of flattening has developed into what he refers to as ''an amusing visual curveball.''[10] As anyone can attest who has encountered the dislocating compressions of such works as *Daisy III* (1980) (cat. 12), *Cow in Space Wrinkle* (1982) (cat. 21), *House Bull* (1982) and *Pet Cow* (1980) (cats. 22 and 23) or the recent *Assyrian Cows* (1987) (cat. 42), such flattening is an arresting formal device. Yet the curveball might also be thought of as a screwball. Underlying much of Fafard's work, and germane to the issue of critical doctrines, is a confrontation of culture and nature. This forms part of the conceptual structure of *Bird* and *DC-Neuf*. The former, seen through the eyes of

22. *House Bull* (1982)
Clay and glaze

23. *Pet Cow* (1980)
Clay and glaze

a bird, involves minimal human intrusion. The latter, with its highway-choked landscape, is a depiction of the ramifications of human culture seen from the vantage point of one of them, a passing airplane. Similarly, even as the physical contortions of a *Cow in Space Wrinkle* carry an implicit comment about the imposition of critical imperatives, they also make residual reference to man's impositions on nature. However pleasing visually, these works are about the effects of playing around with the natural world, a theme made explicit in a group of nine twisted and pancaked ''embryo transplant'' offspring (not included in the exhibition) and their less deformed but nonetheless flattened mother, *Daisy I* (1980) (cat. 11).

A telling counterpoint to Fafard's flattened works and all they can mean is his treatment of the community of local artists with whom he is personally friendly. Unlike Greenberg, who represents reaction, or the early modern European artists to whom he has turned, or even his cows, which are treated as symbols or mythic representations, these figures are played straight. *Jerry* (1984) (cat. 29) and *Russ* (1984) (cat. 30), for example, are fully modelled. They have been caught in characteristic poses with characteristic expressions and a high degree of realistic detail. As part of Fafard's human attachment to the core reality of his place, it would not do to mess with people like these. On them, flatness would fall flat.

P.W.

1. W.H. Auden quoted in Walter Redfern, *Puns* (Oxford: Basil Blackwell Publisher Ltd., 1986), 147.

2. Kay Larson, ''The Dictatorship of Clement Greenberg,'' *Artforum* 25 (Summer 1987): 76.

3. Larson, 77.

4. These longstanding divisions are still keenly felt. During the course of this exhibition, Greenberg is to receive an honorary doctorate from the University of Regina. The decision to so honor Greenberg is seen by some in the Regina art community as reinforcing old wounds.

5. See, for instance, Greenberg's comments about Wassily Kandinsky and Marsden Hartley in Clement Greenberg, *The Collected Essays and Criticism* (vol. 2, *Arrogant Purpose* 1945-1949) ed. John O'Brien (Chicago and London: The University of Chicago Press, 1986), 3.

6. The idea of doing a portrait of Greenberg was suggested initially by Chris Birt of Toronto.

7. Redfern, 125.

8. Redfern, 174.

9. Redfern, 179.

10. Joe Fafard in conversation with the author June 11, 1987.

29. *Jerry* (1984)
Clay, glaze and acrylic paint

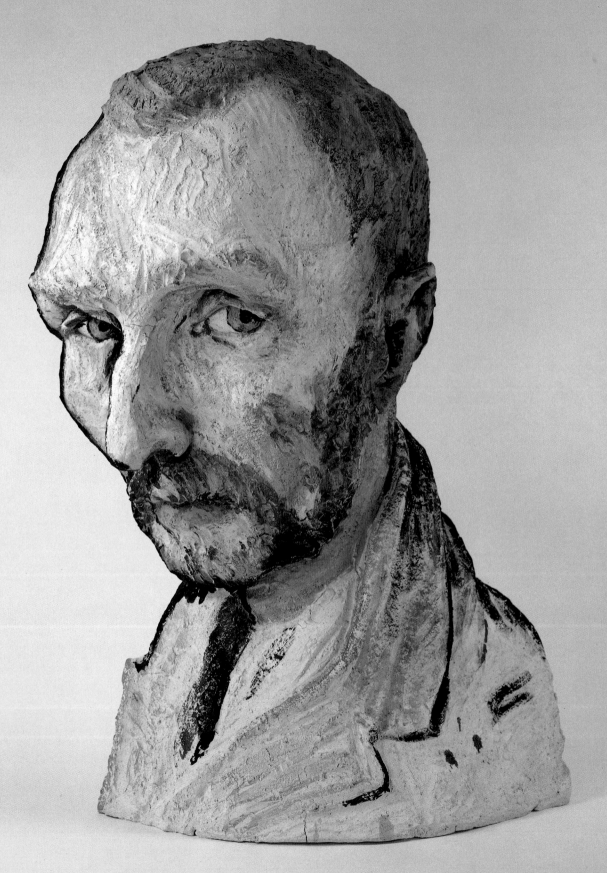

27. *Vincent #4* (1983)
Clay and acrylic paint

R eturn again to the source of the portrait in Fafard's work and what it stands for: an attachment to community, a sense of place. Whatever Fafard's cows, bulls and calves represent, there is a pastoral familiarity suggested which recalls the Pense portraits and the portraits of relatives and friends from the artistic community which Fafard has made since 1973. These Pense portraits affirmed that the rural culture was a viable subject, and a warm counterpoint to the earlier satirical portraits of "art critics and artists and people who play the art game."[1] When, in 1973, Fafard began to reach into the art world again for subject matter, he did so on the affectionate level of the familiar. He portrayed untrained prairie artists – Jan Wyers (1973), Harvey McInnes (1977), and W.C. McCargar (1974) (fig. 7), whose work had "dignity, honesty, integrity and raw motivation" – as well as artists who worked on the same critical edge as he did: David Thauberger (1978) (cat. 4) and Russell Yuristy (1978). In each case he tied himself to artists with strong regional attachments and like-minded sensibilities.

In the late 1970s and without cynical intent, Fafard began to reflect on the larger tradition of which all artists were part. In comments written for a special *artscanada* issue on prairie folk art, he linked the work of folk artist, Jan Wyers, with the abstractions of Mark Rothko, and the paintings of the Maritime folk painter, Joe Sleep, with the work of Picasso. He wrote:

> One is affected by other human beings who are totally genuine in their approach to whatever they're doing and this is the overriding spirit that I find in all good works of art. It is not necessarily limited to folk artists. I see that kind of thing in good painters of the past, present, working any place, anywhere.[2]

His intention was not to create a lineage of direct influence, but to suggest a world of feeling where artistic commitment begins. It was a generalization which led beyond Pense and beyond the artists in his immediate and contemporary community. He had identified with the people of Pense as individuals who were marginalized from the centers of power, yet were self-reliant and assured. And so, he could do just the same with artists who worked with shared values and circumstances in his time, and in other times and other places. In one sense he had done this already. His portraits of *Louis Riel, Gabriel Dumont,* and *Cree Man* (fig. 1), which he did from 1975 through 1979, recalled men who were leaders of defiant communities. They were not of his place, but they were of his culture. He felt bonded to them. These portraits

19. *My Picasso* (1981)
Clay, glaze and acrylic paint

20. *Matisse* (1981)
Clay, glaze and acrylic paint

4. *Dave* (1978)
Clay, glaze and acrylic paint

underline one essential tenet of community value: that the scale of place leads everyone to feel as if they know everyone else. They conjure up a sense of slow motion time – a feeling, not only that a whole life could be lived within a community, but that a community could be that way forever.

In 1980, Fafard's subjects turned to focus on artistic leadership and an international tradition which he revered. His portraits of European artists, Picasso, Matisse, Cézanne and, centrally, van Gogh, were representations of a world of intense creativity. These were Fafard's "friends of the imagination,"[3] artists who, in the past, had looked upon dominant art traditions and communities from the outside, and had questioned existing value.

Picasso's inventive sensibility and his willingness to have fun with certain artistic traditions encouraged homage. As well, Fafard had long admired Picasso's independence. As a Spanish artist who lived most of his creative life in Paris, Picasso had the outsider's take on the dominant art center of the times. There was a parallel here. Matisse was also detached from the controlling metropolis, had also shunned intense scrutiny in the eye of the center, and soaked himself in the Mediterranean light of the French Riviera. His interest in the capacity of art simply to evoke the generous comforts of an armchair contrasted with the words and "artspeak" that encapsulated all art movements and transformed gesture and intuition into manifesto and radical will. It was a questioning Fafard could respond to.

The first of the works – portraits of Picasso and Matisse – followed Fafard's visit to New York to see the Picasso retrospective at The Museum of Modern Art in the summer of 1980. As homages, Fafard's portraits of Picasso and Matisse stand in the tradition of faithful portraiture. *My Picasso* (1981) (cat. 19) and *Matisse* (1981) (cat. 20) share the particularity of the closely observed: the casual drop of the arm, the alert, all-seeing eyes, the well-worn enveloping workman's shroud. The Picasso portrait, in particular, is about personal testament (it has never been for sale), but each is an evocation of a specific, lovingly felt presence, and a chronicle of a work ethic, in the tradition of the Pense portraits.

Fafard's portraits of Picasso and Matisse de-emphasized the experimental qualities of the clay in favor of detailed descriptive modelling. And yet, a playfulness was inherent in the medium. He had explored this playfulness in 1980 with his series of four portraits of the American

(fig. 7) *McCargar* (1974)
Clay, glaze,
acrylic, luster
40.6 × 26.4 × 38.1 cm

critic, Clement Greenberg. He had played with illusion through manipulated perspective, had flattened Greenberg according to formalist principles, and thus had recreated a personality in the image of its own critique. In his 1982 portraits of Vincent van Gogh, Fafard picked up once again the intent to realize portraiture in the personality and formal interests of the subject. Here was a painter to admire for his sense of sculptural volume. The sheer vigor of paint application led Fafard to wonder "what van Gogh would have done had he become a sculptor." It seemed as if the substance of each stroke was like the etcher's incised line, carved and scratched from a surface. For Fafard, van Gogh's work relates itself more directly to a tradition of low relief sculpture than to painting itself, and his interest in van Gogh is, consequently, formally inquisitive. He has chosen to represent van Gogh in the manner and tone of van Gogh's sensibility: strident in color and aggressive in surface.

Fafard's portrait images of van Gogh are in the tradition of *Louis Riel*, and the portrait, *Mon Père* (1972) (fig. 5), which Fafard made of his own father, shortly after his death. They are memorials to his ancestors. Like his homages to Picasso and Matisse, and the Pense portraits before that, the van Gogh works are created from a notion of the ideal. Van Gogh held onto the cherished ideal of founding an artists' colony in the south of France; he had a skepticism about Paris which Fafard admires. Thus, *Dear Vincent* (1983) (cat. 25) represents the earthly van Gogh branding himself into the future with the intensity of his vision, clutching a candle which represents his cherished colleague, Gauguin. It is all symbol and inspiration: van Gogh painted afire with the intense pure colors from his brush – his whole posture accusing the world of abandonment – while holding in his hand the representation of an artistic hopefulness of his own making. Fafard's achievement is to push his own representations of intense belief into the language of an acknowledged master. The high sharp edges of clay in *Vincent #4* (1983) (cat. 27), the twists against the central axis of the body in *The Painter* (1986) (cat. 41), the radiant etching so apparent in many of the *Vincent Self-Portrait Series* (1983-87) (cat. 44) – all reinforce the sense that van Gogh has been absorbed and understood as a bundle of emotions. To capture such intensity has been Fafard's desire. He has wanted, above all, to express his understanding of "those sensations that come to anyone who has pushed."

37

25. *Dear Vincent* (1983)
Clay and acrylic paint

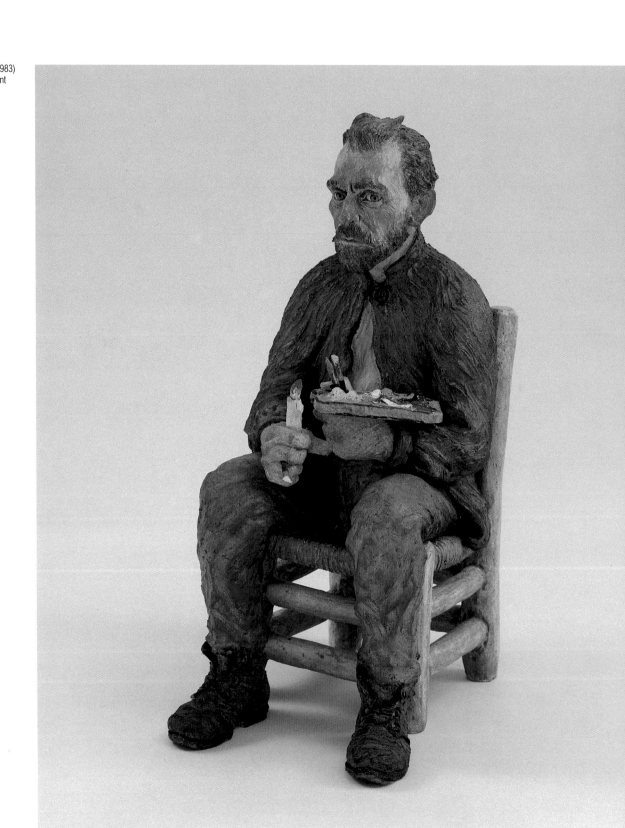

40. *Gauguin* (1986)
Clay, acrylic paint, wood and wicker

Van Gogh's honest expression of deep comitment to "ordinary souls" has embedded itself in Fafard's idea of community. For Fafard, the telling contrast is with Gauguin who journeyed to the South Seas in search of an idyllic tropical civilization. His idea of the "noble savage" led him, in Fafard's view, to a superficial reading of the spiritualism of primitive cultures. There was no empathy with lives of an unknown community, no sense of struggle to be learned from their experience. Gauguin represents primitivism as a form of conquest. When, in 1986, Fafard did his single cynical portrait of *Gauguin* (1986) (cat. 40), he created a private voodoo doll – with no softness or affection. Gauguin's humility of religious posture is betrayed by his naked genitals. For Gauguin, beatitude is a cynical strategy for acceptance, and sexual desire is mere conquest.

If, for Fafard, a central issue is ancestral authority, then it is Cézanne who assumes the role of the true patriarch. Fafard completed a clay bust of Cézanne in 1982, shortly after realizing his portraits of Picasso and Matisse. In 1986, three portraits of Cézanne were made concurrently with portraits of van Gogh. Fafard presents Cézanne as an ancestor figure, in fatherly pose. He is, for example, an artist who encouraged younger artists and pushed personal discovery. His own obsessive experimentation with the image of Mont Sainte-Victoire is a twentieth-century beacon; his obsessive experimentation is a touchstone for modernism. It is also, and pointedly so for Fafard, the evidence of one artist's loyalty to a rural place, a place of personal identification.[4]

Fafard presents Cézanne in various poses, pushing formal ideas to their limit of almost comical extremes. In *Cézanne III* (1986) (cat. 38), Fafard has tipped his hat to Cézanne's own achievement – the representation of mass through ordering of planes – by representing his torso as a series of faceted surfaces. The painted forms, with their open brushstrokes, refer back to Cézanne's own method of working ("passage," the art historians have called it – open brush strokes which blur distinctions of foreground and background space). In their various poses and detail, the portraits of Cézanne highlight Fafard's own interest in explorations of abstracted form. One is full-figure-rounded, another, a flattened illusion of three dimensional form, a third, flattened, tilted forward and further enlarged. Together, as representations of the same subject, they underline Fafard's recognition of Cézanne's own obsessions with the play of formal relationships.

Within his continuing series of artists' portraits, Fafard has placed himself, though not for the first time. In this instance his lineage is historical: figures he could not know except through the personality of the historical sketch. He has identified van Gogh and the others as his community and created them, of course, in the image of his own needs. In a sense, they represent to him emblems of success. They represent ideas or attitudes that are positive reminders of the strength of artistic thought. Fafard creates them to evoke good feeling and objectify his sense of kinship; the process of creating their likeness leads him to understand his subjects more fully. What American critic Donald Kuspit has said of the California ceramic artist Robert Arneson's interest in worldly artists is also true of Fafard's representations: "they are familiarized into colleagues with compulsions."[5]

In moving towards greater and greater formal freedom – in part encouraged by the newly discovered possibilities of cast bronze – Fafard has wandered away from a folk art influence of cherished finishes. In his work, surface handling is generally anxious, and the pose and expression of his subjects reveal a particularity of personality. In doing so, he has, nonetheless, maintained an essentially Romantic sensibility which proposes the ideal as a reflection of what the present can be. Fafard's self-determined, fanciful family tree is carefully chosen, and it continually expands.

M.T.

1. Geoffrey Ursell, "Fafard," *Emerging Arts West* (October 1975): 3.

2. Joe Fafard in Eli Mandel, ed., "A Comprehensible World," *artscanada* 36 (October/November 1979): 19.

3. These and subsequent unattributed quotations are taken from conversations with Joe Fafard in the spring of 1987.

4. Fafard contrasts Cézanne's example with that of Manet, whose scenes of Parisian life suggest little of the particularities of place and no sense of the artist as other than the voyeuristic eye.

5. Donald Kuspit, "Robert Arneson's Sense of Self," *American Craft* (October/November 1986): 44.

38. *Cézanne III* (1986)
Bronze, patina and acrylic paint

32. *Dear Vincent* (1985)
Bronze and patina (1/7)

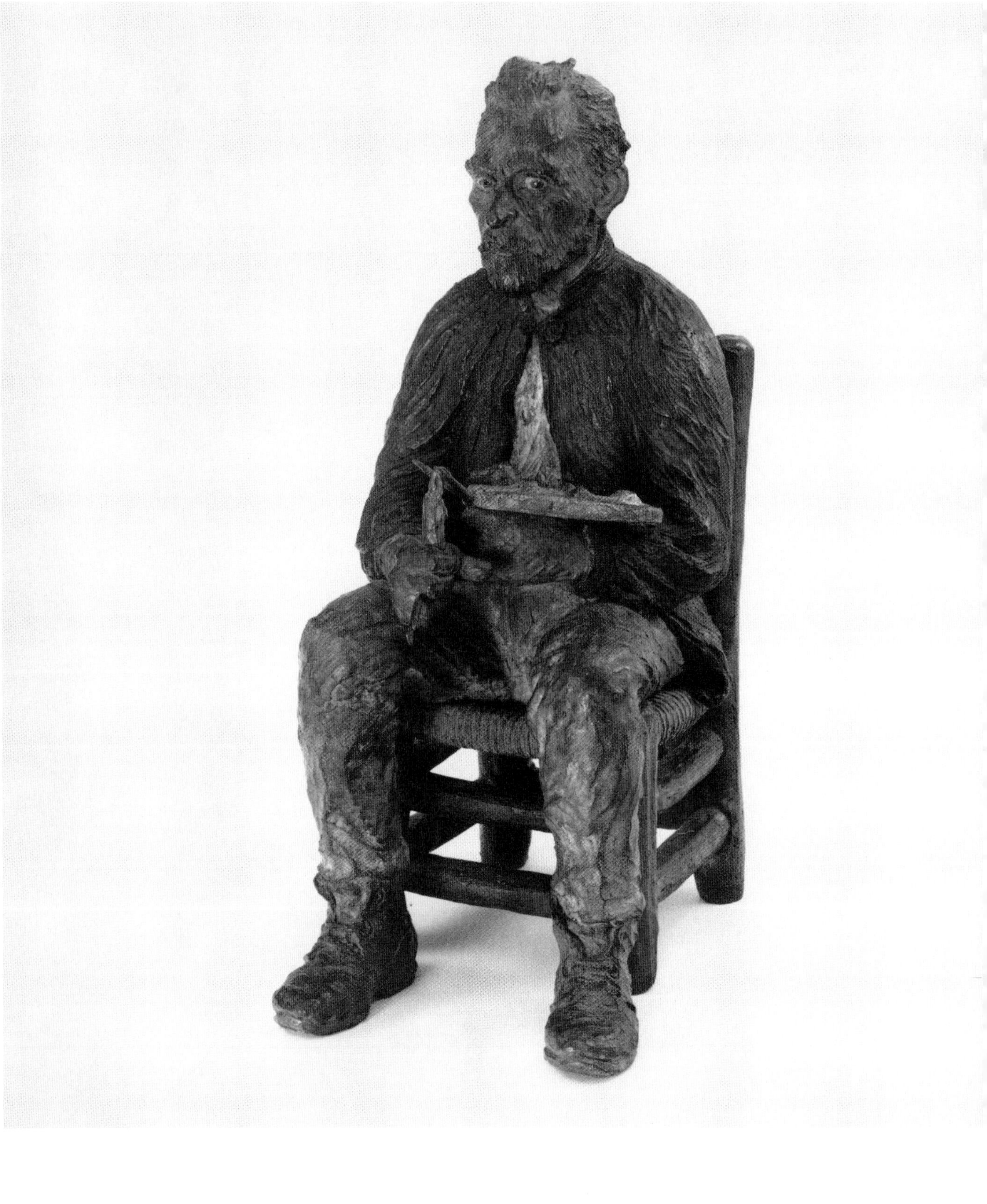

CONCLUSION

In the past ten years Joe Fafard and his work have found larger and larger audiences. He has had commercial exhibitions of a wide variety of work in galleries across the country; in 1985 his large outdoor installation, *The Pasture*, was unveiled with notable fanfare at the Toronto-Dominion Centre in downtown Toronto; he has been profiled in numerous documentary films; and his work has been chronicled in a continually growing file of articles from the popular press. Indeed, in the last few years, it has often seemed as if Fafard has become one of the folk heros he portrayed.

That he has received such popular acclaim while working some distance from the dominant commercial and cultural centers reflects his commitment to issues of regional identity. While neither scornful of nor hostile to the reality of the large metropolises, Fafard has created his own evocative body of work from the strength of apparently marginal communities. Fafard inverts the conventional wisdom that larger centers are more complex, more interesting, and more committed to higher artistic value by working with a populism of emotions and everyday experiences which implicate and involve large audiences.

Cows and Other Luminaries 1977-1987 presents Fafard's recent work as a mid-career survey. With all the acclaim Fafard received for his early body of work, which was original and identifiably his own, he has continued to challenge many of the easily held assumptions about his work. He has done this, in part, through a search for formal aggressiveness which has now begun to find its material expression in bronze. The foundry which Fafard has set up in Pense is part of this mid-career twist. It is a high risk venture, cloaked in the go-for-broke daring of making a frontier project work. In this sense, among others, the foundry builds on Fafard's agrarian roots. It is, at once, a cooperative venture, an embodiment of Fafard's work ethic, and a means to exert individual control over production. At the same time, the self-reflection that has increasingly occupied Fafard has led him to a more public exploration of the meaning of artistic lineage and inspiration. In its earliest stages, the project of portraying important modern European artists was an intensely private one; few were for sale and their isolation in any exhibition was discouraged. In the context of *Cows and Other Luminaries* this has changed, not because Fafard now sees the work differently, but because he has gained the assurance to see his place in relation to it differently.

It is worth noting that, while the critical sympathy the concept of regionalism enjoyed in the seventies and early eighties seems to have abated, life in Saskatchewan goes on. The authority of sheer size cannot be created for small communities anywhere, and a larger scale for this place cannot be manufactured. That Fafard has chosen to work with the realities of a seemingly isolated place, however, is not an ironic comment about limitation. It is, as regionalism is generally, a commitment to community memory as a foundation of a larger historical consciousness. It can be seen, as all regional histories can be seen, as a statement that generalities about Canada's history must come from the basis of clear, experienced fact. It is also a statement that Canada is too big for too many generalizations, anyway.

30. *Russ* (1984)
Clay, glaze and acrylic paint

INTERVIEW

The text which follows is from an interview with Joe Fafard and is meant to provide a chronological framework through which Fafard's various interests and series of works can be approached. The interview took place in Regina, Saskatchewan, on June 30, 1987. It was conducted by Matthew Teitelbaum and Peter White.

Will you make some general comments about your early childhood that might tell us something of your work?

The whole world that I knew consisted only of a small village and a small French-Canadian and Métis community that was centered around the church, the parish and family. The family was a very proud and independent family. My father was a farmer and so was his father. They both lived in the community that I grew up in. We had a tremendous sense of being separate, and you might even call it alienated, from the rest of the community that surrounded us. I had that feeling, I guess, of estrangement and alienation from an early age. We were a very close, independent family and our interaction amongst ourselves was very honest and straightforward. We didn't have a sense of saving each other's feelings. We weren't hard on each other but we were very truthful, and I think that in a way we spent a lot of time examining each other, grooming each other. This gave us a sense of observation that I feel quite keen.

Generally we lived as peasants live at any time. We had a long tradition and culture which was mostly centered around the church. There was the ritual of wearing your best clothes on Sunday and going to church and meeting people and then coming home for dinner after church and inviting a few of the relatives and everybody spending their Sunday afternoons in a very pleasant kind of banter.

There were twelve kids in my family eventually; I was number six. My grandparents lived only about 200 yards from us. I spent a lot of time with my grandmother because she was a rather finicky person and I was one of the few kids in my family who suited her liking. She felt I could come over there and spend the whole afternoon amusing myself with the toys she had or with drawing paper. I didn't disturb her. She told my mother once that she liked me because I didn't fight. My grandmother was a big influence on me. She died when I was eleven.

Your mother made what might be called folk art objects. Was she important for your interest in art?

At that time she didn't have time to do anything called art. It wasn't so much that she was doing art, but she was a person who made anything out of anything. She made practically all the Christmas toys. She made the clothes. The ethics of making things was always part of our lives, and she was naturally an influence because we could see that kind of creativeness going on. It was her ability to make something out of something totally different that was the influence. Just make do, create, whatever, and adapt to whatever situation there was.

Are you aware of a moment when you became interested in making art?

I have no idea about that. Because I had an ability to amuse myself by drawing on paper with pencil or whatever would make a mark, I would carry them everywhere with me. An incident is told in my family: one morning the family, with a few aunts and uncles, was sitting at the table. As I came downstairs I was carrying my pencil and paper. One of the aunts turned around and said, *"Voici, l'artiste Canadien-Français . . .* here's the great

French-Canadian artist coming down for breakfast." From that moment on the tag sort of stuck with me, that I was an artist.

When I started school the teacher and other students felt that I could draw. The first thing I did in school was draw a huge horse on the blackboard in front of the whole school.

We knew no artists. But since the adults seemed to think there was the possibility of someone being an artist – and that person would have to be able to draw – then I liked the idea. I think if you had given me a choice when I was nine years old, I probably would have been Maurice Richard, but that wasn't the case. So I kept on thinking about art right through high school.

When you "made it" to art school, what was it like?

Well, I thought my art education at the University of Manitoba was wonderful. It was virtually the first time that I had an opportunity to share ideas with other young people my age and I really took to it. But the further along I went, especially when I went to Penn State, the less I liked it. It was 1966 to 1968 and I felt really disturbed by the whole political scene in the United States. I felt disturbed, too, by the vastness of it all – so many hundreds of art schools and so many hundreds and thousands of students all going there. It became very machinelike and it no longer had that personal feel to things. I didn't find any teachers there that I could relate to except an art historian. I didn't like those two years in Pennsylvania.

What art did you see there?

I saw a lot of art. I travelled often to New York. We hung around at the Whitney and the Metropolitan, and The Museum of Modern Art. I went to a lot of the commercial shows at the Leo Castelli gallery and we talked a lot, but it wasn't all that satisfying to me. I found the art too cerebral, not enough what I would call

personal guts in the work. Here I'm thinking of the work of Robert Morris – his cut-up carpets and things like that. In my own work, I toyed with all those things – with minimalism and kinetic art – and I really floundered around trying to find what I wanted to do or how to make sense of it all. As students, we were very concerned with the question of "what is art?"

There seem to be few published references to your early work. Could you describe some of the pieces that you made at that time?

The first things I did at Penn State were large plaster figures. I did three or four within the first two months that I was there. My studio teacher was Italo Scanga. He really hated the things I was doing and gave me a bad time. He called my stuff sentimental, romantic, and things like that. There were other students there, some from New York, and the joke was me. I had a hard time there for a while. One day I just took all the figures I had made and put them in the middle of the floor and broke them all up. I left them there in a pile and went away for a couple of days. When I came back, I went into pottery and worked there for a while. I tried to reconstruct what I wanted to do by exploring a lot of other things but they didn't make a great deal of sense to me. Then one day, as I was sitting at the breakfast table, a big tall highchair popped into my mind. So that's what I did – I built this gigantic highchair. I could sit in it and be the kid that I was. Whoever wanted to sit in it could recapture that feeling of precariously looking down at the ground. After that I started making kinetic foam rubber things. I also made a number of large plaster figures. I think I made about four or five, which I left completely white. They were portraits of various individuals in the art department. I had those in a show that the students put together.

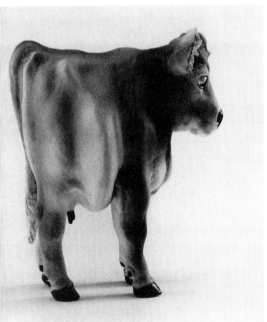

12. *Daisy III* (1980)
Clay and glaze

They were quite well received but I denied them as art objects. During my graduate interview, some of the professors tried to point out that these figures were really what my work should be, but I rejected that and insisted that my real art was the kinetic work. When I came to Regina, I left all those figures there and brought back the kinetic work and the highchair.

Would you describe some of the kinetic pieces?

They vibrated and just moved slowly around. It was almost frightening to see these animated dead objects. They used to frighten the kids a lot. I had a flying french fry and an animated palm tree that would twirl around. I also had a side-winder which was a long piece of foam rubber with a motor inside. The rod was bent and the motor turned the rod. The thing would take off in shapes that undulated and crawled around on the floor. I also had a large box with five engines hanging from it. It was held up by the shaft that turned it so this thing would sort of creep around another box with tentacles hanging over it, sort of feeling the box below it. I did like those things. I still do actually. But I didn't enjoy being an engineer and working out the problems of making them work.

How was it that you came to Regina in 1968?

Well, I wanted to come back. I felt I had made a promise, in a sense, to come back because I had received a Saskatchewan Arts Board grant to go away to study and I had said that I would come back. I wanted a job and I got one in Regina.

How did things go that first year?

That first year, while teaching, I was trying to get my own work together but it wasn't coming. I felt quite inadequate as a teacher because my own work was suffering so much. By the end of the year I had decided to quit but then I came in contact with David Gilhooly's work. Suddenly I realized it really didn't matter what you did as long as you did something that you felt was engaging, and you didn't have to bother with this very heavy cerebral question about making "art." I decided to go back to making things but using only those things that are the most simple to use, that is, my hands and some liquid plaster. That's when I started doing busts about two feet high of colleagues at the university: Ted Godwin, Jack Sures, Russ Yuristy, Terry Marner, Ric Gomez and David Gilhooly.

Were they people you were close to or were they people who just provided easy access to subject matter?

Well, I certainly felt close to some of them, especially to Russ Yuristy. He's the first one that I did. I felt close enough to Jack Sures. About subject matter: when I decided to switch my work I didn't want any interruption so I changed studios and went into a basement studio in the old sculpture building. I got a lock for the door and didn't allow anyone in my studio for two or three months. I did one piece and set it aside, and then did another one. They were busts with plaster on them – wood plate with just a metal rod. I painted them fairly roughly. I was just trying to get a sense of the presence of those people and their most common expression and demeanor. During one noon hour when everybody was away, I set the work on pedestals along the hallways of the art school. When people came back from lunch, they were suddenly confronted with a whole display or show of themselves. My idea was to do

42. *Assyrian Cows* (1987)
Bronze and patina

something that people could see and relate to without the question of "art" coming up. I wanted these things – which people called the "rogues' gallery" – to appear suddenly out of the blue and function as an amusing event. The rogues' gallery was not really the beginning but a coming back to what I could do. I had been doing things like that while I was a student in Winnipeg and I had done a few at Pennsylvania and they were always the things that gave me the most joy. Somehow, in those days, I wasn't confident enough to say this is where I am and stick to it. I wanted to try to find out about the art that people were talking about: why was it that such stuff was displayed in Leo Castelli's gallery? So it was, I guess, humility and wanting to know that kept me falling off my own track.

Was Gilhooly teaching in the department at this time?

Yes. I had gone to one of his talks where he showed the world of frogs and I really enjoyed it. It was really one of Gilhooly's finer moments. I realized that art could be that simple, that much joy and fun, and that's what I wanted to do.

So Gilhooly's message to you was not "this is the kind of work you should do," but rather "the kind of work you feel comfortable with is a valid thing to do."

That's right.

What else was going on in the art community? What was the influence of David Zack [an art writer from California, who was living in Regina at that time]?

David Zack was an influence for a time. We were always amazed at how he took art seriously – seriously in the sense that he thought that everything people did in art had meaning and sense and that its soul was revealing. If you'd say,

"Wouldn't it be crazy to do this?" and it would be the most outrageous thing, he thought we meant it. And then he'd go about the steps of doing it, of planning and carrying it out. David Zack thought that anything you thought could be turned into reality. So, in a way, he was an influence because he broadened all kinds of possibilities instead of just sticking to what seemed reasonable, practical things to do. David Zack thought that if you thought of it, it was as good as done. You could go ahead and carry it through. He was an influence in the sense that he was such a wild card. He gave the place an aura of zaniness. You could just be as zany as you wanted to be.

Following the rogues' gallery, you commited yourself more and more to ceramic portraiture. What were some of the works you did following your move to Pense in December of 1971?

Prior to moving I had done a portrait of a 107-year-old man, Michael Haynee. About two weeks into January of 1972 my father died. I started his portrait some time after that. I continued doing portraits like *George*, the portraits of my in-laws, of *Groszmama*, my uncle *Charlie*, my mother. When I started those portraits I had to go back and review or re-encapsulate my own past. When I started the portraits it was a sort of therapy. I was going back and gathering all those things unto myself that I had known, and bringing them all back. The family came first, because I was trying to penetrate those layers, outwardly. Eventually it involved the community of Pense because of the new friends I was making there. I felt the community of Pense was a new, larger family – the one I left a long time before.

What eventually brought about your leaving the university in 1974? What were your feelings about art and about the university at that time?

I felt that we were isolated in the university, that we were an academic body which really didn't care to associate much with the community. Stuff like that. There were art department politics and personal things which led me to leave. My father died in 1972 and my sister died in 1973 and then in 1974, when my brother was dying, I found myself searching again. It was sort of personal, but it made me consider important things: the brevity of life and how you can squander it, waste it.

In all of this, how do the cows fit in? What was your interest in doing them and how do you see them in relation to the portraits made at this time?

I had done the rogues' gallery in 1969, followed by a series of standing figures. I started sharing a studio with Gilhooly and he was constantly making animal things. He worked in clay and I used plaster and we had to keep fairly separate from each other because the two materials don't mix at all. But one day I picked up some of his clay and I made a couple of cows. Gilhooly took them home with him and fired them for me, brought them back, and I put some glazes on them. He took them home and fired them again. I was really disgusted with the garishness of the things and he said, ''Don't criticize it. You just have to accept what is given to you. You made them. You have no right to refuse what the kiln-god (or whatever he was referring to) has granted you.'' I thought that was quite interesting but I really didn't think that I would go on to make very many cows. During the summer, when Gilhooly was away in California, David Thauberger and I worked a lot in the art school. I had a studio there and David was a student in the ceramic department. We made a whole bunch of stuff and were very

excited about being able to show it to Gilhooly when he got back from California. He had become the guru, and although I was a member of the staff, I was just like one of the students at that point. I showed my things to Gilhooly and he had a strange reaction this time: ''No, those aren't very good.'' Somehow that got me trying harder, trying to get a little more pizzazz into the things. It eventually worked to the point where the cows became something like a pilot project for experimenting with the clay, for feeding my technique into the figures. The point of it was that it was no longer a subject but more a form that you continued to develop and experiment with. That has continued all the way through, from that point on.

Did you think the cows, in the sense that you're talking about them, related to Gilhooly's frogs?

I don't think so. The thinking at the time was that everyone should choose a motif. Gilhooly obviously had his frogs cornered. When he saw that I made cows, he said, ''Trust you to pick as dumb an animal as a cow as your motif.'' I said, ''I don't understand. I didn't pick the cow as my motif. That's not what it's about.'' What it was about for me was to speak of those things that I knew, that hark back to that community and those days when my perception was developed back on the farm. I just wanted to bring that out.

By the time you stopped doing the Pense portraits you had begun a series of historical figures, and portraits of people who weren't, apparently, connected to Pense. What made you feel you were finished with Pense?

I never felt I was finished with Pense. I always intended to do a number of portraits that I never did do. When I moved away from doing those things, it wasn't to abandon them so much as to be able to pick up more vocabulary – get

24. *Buck Fighting for Doe* (1983)
Clay, glaze and lusters with lamp fixture

more into my art. The last portraits in Pense are far back – as far back as 1974 or 1975. Later I was doing portraits of close friends, like Russ Yuristy and David Thauberger. This for me is not so separate from Pense. My community is not just a small town. It gets to be larger and larger. In 1980, for example, I did a portrait of Margaret Laurence. To me she was just like someone I knew. I had a profound respect for her so she became part of my community. In a sense, I continued doing the Pense portraits but in a different community. I gathered about me different people. The historical figures have the same motivation as the portraits of my family. I was trying to bring all my past unto myself. The historical figures are our small collective past. Louis Riel and the people who lived at the same time as Crowfoot and Big Bear are certainly important figures. To me these were exotic people. These were illiterate people; they didn't have the art of writing English or French; they didn't have the art of signage. I was fascinated by a human mind that related directly to its environment without a great deal of filtering. I felt these people projected upon their environment with their imagination or by mythic stories and I felt the need to think about an intelligence that relates to its environment in a direct kind of way.

Another extension of community, perhaps a perverse one, includes the portraits you did of Clement Greenberg in 1980. Would you see him, in some odd kind of way, as being part of your sense of community, of your own experience?

Well, he wasn't part of the community as I try to define community; but he was perhaps the anti-community, the "anti-Christ" of that community, the figure that fractures the community. I feel that Clem's influence in Saskatchewan has been destructive of our creative spirit,

because as doctrine it has plastered and papered over our own sensibility. It seeks to prevent us from feeling our own self and expressing that which is really ourself.

How did the portraits of Greenberg come about?

I had photographs around for a long time. I gave Clem some thought. When I decided to go ahead and do a portrait, I did a small full-standing study first, then a larger version. I did one of his head, at a time when I had been experimenting with foreshortening in my cows. I wanted to experiment and explore how I would translate foreshortening to a flat bust. Later I did a whole bunch of other ones, but they were never as successful as that one portrait of Clem. In 1982 I brought it into the art world with Cézanne and van Gogh and there I was able to give it some life because I was sticking it onto art rather than onto reality.

You also consistently work in other media such as prints and paintings, ceramic tableaux, "lampscapes," ceramic postcards. How do you see those kinds of works in relation to the sculpture you've done?

Well, for me they're what my work is: a form of amusement, a form of how to pass my time, surprise myself, just take delight in doing something and discovering something else. I always think of these works as adding to my vocabulary of tricks and things I can do or that I want to do. So, for example, I did those lamps because landscapes are difficult to do in sculpture. There are very few landscapes done in sculpture that can be called sculpture. What people do is usually put sculpture in landscape but not the other way around. Since the problem of making a landscape is usually that it's a surface upon which you put some objects, I wanted to make an object with very little surface but with a great illusion of depth in terms of space. Those lamps had a mirrored-type background that can go on ad infinitum. I haven't done any of these ''lampscapes'' since I did that series. I don't know why because I'd still like to do some. But it always seems as if there's something else that I want to do.

For the last number of years you have been working in bronze. What brought about the interest in that medium?

I think the same reason that interested me in ceramics in the first place. Because I didn't know it and I always try to find another way to renew my interest and curiosity. I was finding things were getting more outrageous and I was desperate to spark my interest . . . .

What are you thinking about specifically?

Well, I was thinking of those ''lampscapes.'' That might have been the reason I did those – to try and arouse my curiosity. When I was doing my figures, I felt that they were becoming less necessary, less urgent, because I really wasn't able to search out new things, new ways of doing them. They had started to disappear on me. I was looking for a much more gestural, direct way of handling the figure. Within that area, I started working on the van Gogh figures which were really quite opposite from that smooth skin effect that I had been working with up to that point. The bronze things began quite innocently enough, the same way as when I started playing with clay.

How would you talk about the change in the feel, or the rendering of the figures, now that they're being done in bronze?

I don't think I've reached that point yet where I can really decide how this is influencing my way of working. I'm starting to get a feel for the thinness of the material because when I work with clay I usually work thick. Bronze is so shallow and hard that it's practically unbreakable. It can be destroyed but breakage is not a problem so it's starting to allow for lots of long thin shapes and connections that I would never have dared in clay.

But for me the significance is not so much the change from clay to bronze as the change from working by myself to working with five other people and working with machinery that has so much power and requires so much preparation. I feel as if I've bought a brand new combine and am learning to use it and finding that it can thresh so much more than my old stick.

You moved back to Regina in 1984. Initially, the foundry was going to be set up there, but it worked out that you went back to Pense with it. Have you found the connection to the community of Pense is still important to you?

Well, not in terms of my work. It's still important to me because it's there and because I spent so much time there and have so many good memories of it. I still know many people there. Now it's the seat of my business. On the level of my work, I guess I never think about it much anymore, or look to it in the way I looked to it in the past.

Terry Heath pointed out in his 1979 catalogue essay, The Formalism of Fafard, *how much popular literature has been produced about your work without a hard, critical look being taken. With the exception of Vic Cicansky, none of the other artists working in clay in this country seems to have been the subject of sustained enquiry. What do you think that's about?*

I don't know what it's about. Maybe our work is difficult to talk about. Maybe we don't leave much room for anything to be said about it. Maybe it takes a much longer time to be able to talk about it. I haven't felt that this has been a detriment. I've felt that it has been rather nice to have all this time, these years, to work without having to come to that point of constant scrutiny. I've felt pretty well free to go on and just do my work, but maybe that eventually brings one into a void if one continues in that line.

Do you think the popularity of your work somehow makes it difficult for some to take it seriously?

Yes, and the word accessible has been that reason – you don't have to talk about it because it's accessible. Perhaps little has been said because the work has been rather popular and people might think that it can't be any good if it's popular. Maybe they're right. I don't know. I've never found that a problem.

Perhaps a related aspect of this is the fact that you, and numbers of other artists here, always felt you were moving along in a very particular direction, for lack of a better word, that you were involved in what was generally understood to be avant-garde activity. Yet there are others who have not seen it that way. Could you talk about how you felt?

We had gone and investigated the so-called avant-garde, and didn't find openings that really satisfied us spiritually, emotionally, intellectually. For me, the more it was touted as avant-garde, the less avant-garde I felt it to be. If it looks avant-garde, you can be sure it's not; fashion is a detriment to art. When you're talking about that kind of little roller that rolls along called "the avant-garde," which has to keep spinning to map and flatten out the area behind it for others, then I sort of draw the line and say, no, that's not what it's about. Avant-garde is

being perceptive and human and reaching into one's society and trying to pull some meaning and significance out of it for those who are also interested. By rejecting that kind of stylistic, fashionable commodity that's constantly being swallowed and digested by our institutions, we felt, at least I did, that we were avant-garde. The avant-garde is, as someone has said, so vulgar that it's not even recognized as art; we were not recognized as making art at all, and we had no pretense to it; we could care less.

You've said in the past that you look at the quality of work – period. You're not interested, for example, in distinctions between "folk art" and "high art." Is there anything you want to add, in the context of what you've just said about the avant-garde, about certain things you've found in folk art?

I'm talking about that liberty which allows you to forge ahead and do it the way you want and the way you see it, the liberty to take those things that may not be of universal significance to all but are real for you, and shamelessly bring them forward even though they might appear very personal or sentimental. Those are certainly things that determine the attitude of a folk artist – there's absolutely no concern for any of this other stuff. He just goes ahead and gathers from his own sensibility and experience and puts it out there. It may be that he intends it as an historical document, as Fred Moulding does, or it might be something like Collins Eisenhauer did in Nova Scotia, with dancers suggesting the erotic, mythical overtones of sexuality in the Garden of Eden. They are really being very open and personal at the same time. It's not the way you wield a stick but why you would take that freedom to just wield a stick if that's what you want to do. That's where the connection is.

Would you make any generalizations about how the past and the present start to function in your work? Do you see that as an issue in any sense?

For me, it started happening about 1975 with such portraits as *Crowfoot* and *Cree Man* and it continued, and accelerated, to the portraits of van Gogh and Cézanne. I see those as the same things. I don't see the portraits of Cézanne and van Gogh as portraits like those I did of these other artists that are living today. But they are mythic figures in my mind, the same way as the Indians were. I haven't really thought of it as the past and the present. It's very difficult to understand the present anyway, and it's always disappearing.

Do you think your own portraits of van Gogh have chronicled the past?

No. My interest, generally, was selfish. I just wanted to spend some time with a friend of mine and just be able to meditate on certain things. I read all the letters. It was a self-learning, a self-teaching period of time – a time to explore things and to evoke a certain presence in my studio and to think.

At the same time, by doing portraits of van Gogh and Cézanne, Picasso and Gauguin, you worked yourself into a tradition – you placed yourself inside a tradition, no matter how far away in time that tradition was.

I don't see that. I don't think I worked in a tradition.

Maybe tradition isn't the right word. But if you're creating these images in your studio in Pense and making this strong identification with them, then you're placing yourself amongst them.

Oh no, I certainly don't see that as what I did. To me, these are real people who lived at a different time, in a place far, far away. So I'm not trying to place myself within this or that tradition when I do a portrait of van Gogh. I see myself rather as paying a kind of homage to this particular guy, who was the originator of this marvelous work.

44. *Vincent Self-Portrait Series* (1983-87) (detail) Clay and acrylic paint

(fig. 8) Joe Fafard's studio, Pense, 1982

BIOGRAPHY/BIBLIOGRAPHY

Joe Fafard was born September 2, 1942, in Ste. Marthe, Saskatchewan. He attended the University of Manitoba, Winnipeg (B.F.A. 1966), Pennsylvania State University, State College (M.F.A. 1968); was an instructor in sculpture, University of Saskatchewan, Regina, from 1968 to 1974; and visiting lecturer in sculpture, University of California at Davis, winter semester 1980-81. He is the recipient of numerous awards, including the Order of Canada (officer) in 1981 and the Royal Architectural Institute of Canada Allied Arts Award in 1987. From 1971 to 1984 Fafard lived in Pense, Saskatchewan; in 1984 he moved to Regina where he currently resides. In 1985 he opened a foundry, Julienne Atelier Inc., in Pense.

SELECTED SOLO EXHIBITIONS

1970
Exhibition of Local Talent: Fafard and Others, Dunlop Art Gallery, Regina, Saskatchewan

1971
Joe Fafard, Davis Art Center, Davis, California

1972
Joe Fafard: Ceramic Pictures, Alberta College of Art Gallery, Calgary, Alberta (catalogue)

1973
Joe Fafard, University of Alberta Art Gallery and Museum, Edmonton, Alberta
Joe Fafard's Pensées, Winnipeg Art Gallery, Winnipeg, Manitoba (catalogue; travelled)

1974
Joe Fafard, Sheridan Gallery, Sheridan College, Mississauga, Ontario

1975
Joe Fafard, Town Hall, Pense, Saskatchewan
Joe Fafard, Espace 5, Montreal, Quebec

1977
Joe Fafard, Thomas Gallery, Winnipeg
Joe Fafard, Downstairs Gallery, Edmonton

1979
Joe Fafard, Kesik Gallery, Regina
Joe Fafard, Downstairs Gallery, Edmonton
Joe Fafard, Recent Sculpture, Edmonton Art Gallery (catalogue; essay by Terrence Heath; travelled)

1980
Joe Fafard, Candy Store Gallery, Folsom, California
Daisy I and Her Embryo Transplants, Downstairs Gallery, Edmonton
Joe Fafard, Susan Whitney Gallery, Regina
Joe Fafard [and. . .], Gallery Moos, Toronto, Ontario (catalogue; essay by Patrick Lane)

1982
Joe Fafard, Thomas Gallery, Winnipeg
Joe Fafard, Galerie Don Stewart, Montreal
Joe Fafard, Susan Whitney Gallery, Regina

1983
Joe Fafard, Swift Current National Exhibition Centre, Swift Current, Saskatchewan (brochure)
Open Secrets, Woltjen/Udell Gallery, Edmonton
Joe Fafard, Brian Melnychenko Gallery, Winnipeg

1984
Joe Fafard, Susan Whitney Gallery, Regina

1985
Joe Fafard: A Survey, Diane Farris Gallery, Vancouver, British Columbia

1986
Joe Fafard: New Bronze Cows, Woltjen/Udell Gallery Edmonton
Joe Fafard, Gallery Moos, Toronto
Drawing in Sand, Joe Moran Gallery, Regina

1987
Joe Fafard, Susan Whitney Gallery, Regina

17. *New Veau* (1980)
Screenprint (3/70)

1970
Survey/Sondage 70/Realism(e)s, Musée des Beaux Arts, Montreal, Quebec (brochure; travelled)
Joe Fafard and Bev Kelly, Moose Jaw Art Gallery, Moose Jaw, Saskatchewan
Third Annual Regina Invitational, Norman Mackenzie Art Gallery, Regina, Saskatchewan
Saskatchewan: Saskatoon and Regina, Kitchener-Waterloo Art Gallery, Kitchener-Waterloo, Ontario (catalogue; travelled [circulated by The Art Gallery of Ontario, Toronto])

1972
Realism: Emulsion and Omission, Agnes Etherington Arts Centre, Kingston, Ontario (catalogue)
The Cup Show, David Stuart Galleries, Los Angeles, California

1973
Ceramic Objects, Art Gallery of Ontario and New York Cultural Center, New York, New York (brochure)
Canada Trajectoires 73, Musée d'Art Moderne de la Ville de Paris, Paris, France (catalogue)
The Sensible Cup International Exhibition, Kanazawa City, Japan (catalogue)

1974
Ceramiques de Victor Cicansky, Joe Fafard, David Gilhooly, Espace 5, Montreal
Fired Sculpture, The Art Gallery of Greater Victoria, Victoria, British Columbia (catalogue)

1976
Messages From Southern Saskatchewan, Dalhousie University Art Gallery, Halifax, Nova Scotia (catalogue)

1978
Certain Traditions: Recent British and Canadian Art, Edmonton Art Gallery, Alberta (catalogue; travelled)

1980
Pluralities 1980 Pluralités, The National Gallery of Canada, Ottawa, Ontario (catalogue; essay by Philip Fry)
The Continental Clay Connection, Norman Mackenzie Art Gallery, Regina (catalogue)

1981
Vic Cicansky and Joe Fafard, Candy Store Gallery, Folsum, California
Issues in Clay: Western Canadian Sculpture, organized and circulated by Latitude 53 Society of Artists, Edmonton (catalogue)

1982
Vic Cicansky/Joe Fafard, London Regional Art Gallery, London, Ontario (brochure)

1983
5 From Saskatchewan, Canada House, London, England (catalogue; travelled)

1985
Saskatchewan Heritage 1985, Saskatchewan Legislature Building, Regina (brochure; travelled)
The Artists' Choice, Rosemont Art Gallery, Regina
Do You Take This Seriously? Glenbow Museum, Calgary, Alberta

1986
Human Touch, A Touch of Fever: From Canada to Belgium, Le Botonique, Brussels, Belgium (catalogue; travelled)

SELECTED BIBLIOGRAPHY

Ball, Denise. "Joe Fafard: Home-Grown Celebrity in Culture Circles." *The Regina Leader-Post,* January 15, 1981: 23.

Bodolai, Joe. "Masters of Naive Art, Joe Fafard: One Man's Private Prairie Album." *Saturday Night,* vol. 90, no. 6 (November 1975): 30.

Borsa, Joan. "Joe Fafard." *Vanguard,* vol. 14, no. 1 (February 1985): 32.

Burnett, Marilyn. "Fafard, Joseph" in *The Canadian Encyclopedia.* Edmonton: Hurtig Publishers Ltd., 1985: 610.

Butula, Sharon. "Joe Fafard Sets Up His Own Exhibition." *The Regina Leader-Post,* February 10, 1983: C4.

Campbell, Anne. "Recent Work by Joe Fafard." *The Regina Leader-Post,* November 12, 1982: A16.

Caron, Louis. "Mon amis Joe Fafard et ses étranges sculptures." *La Presse,* 7 février, 1976.

Fudge, Paul. "Twists, Surprises at Whitney Show." *The Regina Leader-Post,* November 21, 1980: 52.

Gilchrist, Mary. "Fafard Gives Shape to Subject's Spirit." *Western People,* no. 39 (January 24, 1980): 2-3.

Harrison, May. "Art For Life's Sake." *Chimo!* vol. 2, no. 3 (May 1979): 23-26.

Heath, Terrence. "The Regina Ceramists" *artscanada,* vol. 30, no. 2 (Spring 1973): 68.

—. "The Figure of Fafard." *Brick* (Fall 1985).

—. "Pensive Turtle." *artscanada,* vol. 32, no. 2 (Autumn 1974): 74-75.

Henker, Barbara. "How Now, Bronze Cow?" *Alberta Report,* vol. 13, no. 10 (February 24, 1986): 52-53.

Jonson, Andrew. "The Down-to-Earth Art of Joe Fafard." *Reader's Digest,* vol. 112, no. 673 (May 1, 1978): 169-174.

Mandel, Eli. "A Comprehensible World: The World of Cicansky, Thauberger, Yuristy and Fafard." *artscanada,* vol. 36, no. 3 (October/November 1979): 15-19.

Mays, John Bentley. "NGC Show Doesn't Merit The Barbs." *The Globe and Mail,* July 12, 1980: E11.

—. "Things Are Looking Up For Public Art." *The Globe and Mail,* November 23, 1985: D17.

McConnathy, Dale. "Artist's Image of Himself." *artscanada,* vol. 32, no. 3 (Autumn 1979): 50-54.

McConnell, Clyde. "Two Regina Artists: Fafard and Lambert-Kelly." artscanada, vol. 27, no. 5 (October/November 1970): 79.

—. "Some Thoughts – Theoretical and Practical – On The Gifts Artists Make . . ." *artscanada,* vol. 27, no. 6 (December 1970/January 1971): 36-40.

Russell, Nancy. "Famous Folks Visit Mendel." *The Saskatoon Star-Phoenix,* December 22, 1979: F16.

Shuebrook, Ron. "Regina Funk." *Art and Artists,* vol. 8, no. 5 (August 1973): 39-41.

Ursell, Geoffrey. "Joe Fafard." *Emerging Arts West,* vol. 1, no. 1 (October 1975): 30-35.

Visions: Contemporary Art in Canada. ed. Robert Bringhurst, Geoffrey James, Russell Keziere and Doris Shadbolt. Vancouver/Toronto: Douglas & McIntyre, 1983.

Wilkin, Karen. "Sculpture" in *The Canadian Encyclopedia.* Edmonton: Hurtig Publishers Ltd., 1985: 1665-67.

Zack, David. "Letter From Regina." *Craft Horizons,* vol. 31, no. 3 (June 1971): 62.

—. "3 Contemporains/Fafard . . ." *Vie des Arts,* no. 64 (Autumn 1971): 42-45.

Zwarun, Suzanne. "That Artist Fella." *Maclean's,* vol. 90, no. 15 (July 25, 1977): 22-28.

WORKS IN THE EXHIBITION

28. *Jane* (1984)
Clay, glaze and acrylic paint

Dimensions are in centimeters;
height precedes width, precedes depth.

1. *Baby Bull* 1977
Clay, glaze and acrylic paint
33.6 × 44.3 × 15.1
Collection of David and Veronica Thauberger,
Regina

2. *Bird* 1977
Screenprint (32/100)
44.1 × 59.8 (image); 50.7 × 65.7 (sheet)
Courtesy of the artist

3. *Petit Veau Blanc* 1977
Clay, glaze and acrylic paint
21.1 × 42.9 × 24.5
Collection of Susan Whitney, Regina

4. *Dave* 1978
Clay, glaze and acrylic paint
21.9 × 34.8 × 37.3
Collection of David and Veronica Thauberger,
Regina

5. *DC—Neuf* 1978
Screenprint (31/65)
65.3 × 46.1 (image); 73.2 × 56.7 (sheet)
Courtesy of the artist

6. *Bull* 1979
Clay, glaze and acrylic paint
28.9 × 49.3 × 21.4
Private collection

7. *Bust of Clem* 1980
Clay and acrylic paint
30.2 × 22.1 × 17.5
Collection of Don McVeigh, Ottawa

8. *Calf* 1980
Clay and glaze
68.8 × 43.2 × 28.7
Private collection

9. *Ceramic Bull* 1980
Clay, glaze and acrylic paint
29.4 × 69.0 × 43.5
Collection of the Mendel Art Gallery,
Saskatoon. Purchased with funds from
The Canada Council Special Purchase
Assistance Programme 1980

10. *Clem* 1980
Clay, glaze and acrylic paint
74.3 × 29.1 × 17.5
Private collection

11. *Daisy I* 1980
Clay and glaze
69.5 × 63.0 × 26.7
Collection of Sheelagh Lebovich,
London, United Kingdom

12. *Daisy III* 1980
Clay and glaze
35.3 × 29.2 × 20.6
Collection of Mayo Graham, Ottawa

13. *Flat Hereford* 1980
Clay and glaze
39.6 × 31.4 × 12.8
Private collection

14. *Huh!* 1980
Clay, glaze and acrylic paint
34.9 × 66.4 × 19.5
Courtesy of the artist

15. *Model of Clem* 1980
Clay and acrylic paint with wooden base
22.5 × 9.6 × 6.9
Collection of Vic Cicansky, Craven,
Saskatchewan

16. *My Art Critic* 1980
Clay and acrylic paint
60.0 × 37.1 × 20.5
Courtesy of the artist

17. *New Veau* 1980
Screenprint (3/70)
47.9 × 47.5 (image); 58.2 × 56.0 (sheet)
Courtesy of the artist

18. *Pieta* 1980
Screenprint (28/60)
49.3 × 63.0 (image); 58.6 × 73.6 (sheet)
Courtesy of the artist

19. *My Picasso* 1981
Clay, glaze and acrylic paint
46.1 × 26.3 × 33.5
Courtesy of the artist

20. *Matisse* 1981
Clay, glaze and acrylic paint
58.5 × 41.6 × 40.4
Courtesy of Woltjen/Udell Gallery,
Edmonton

21. *Cow in Space Wrinkle* 1982
Clay and glaze
37.1 × 23.4 × 30.6
Private collection
Courtesy of Woltjen/Udell Gallery,
Edmonton

22. *House Bull* 1982
Clay and glaze
43.6 × 77.3 × 22.2
Private collection

23. *Pet Cow* 1980
Clay and glaze
40.7 × 56.8 × 10.4
Private collection

24. *Buck Fighting for Doe* 1983
Clay, glaze and lusters with lamp fixture
38.5 × 43.6 × 25.0
Collection of Sheelagh Lebovich,
London, United Kingdom

25. *Dear Vincent* 1983
Clay and acrylic paint
63.4 × 26.2 × 40.7
Courtesy of the artist

26. *Untitled* 1983
Clay, glaze and lusters with lamp fixture
33.5 × 32.2 × 16.5
Private collection

27. *Vincent #4* 1983
Clay and acrylic paint
83.9 × 56.4 × 24.9
Collection of The Canadian Broadcasting
Corporation, Regina

28. *Jane* 1984
Clay, glaze and acrylic paint
45.8 × 14.2 × 24.3
Private collection.
Courtesy of Susan Whitney Gallery, Regina

29. *Jerry* 1984
Clay, glaze and acrylic paint
39.2 × 22.5 × 39.6
Collection of Mr. and Mrs. James Slater,
Toronto

30. *Russ* 1984
Clay, glaze and acrylic paint
38.1 × 29.4 × 30.5
Collection of J. Ron Longstaffe, Vancouver

31. *Vic* 1984
Clay, glaze and acrylic paint
48.3 × 27.5 × 31.4
Private collection.
Courtesy of Susan Whitney Gallery, Regina

32. *Dear Vincent* 1985
Bronze and patina (1/7)
63.9 × 27.3 × 39.9
Private collection.
Courtesy of Susan Whitney Gallery, Regina

33. *Untitled* 1985
Bronze and patina (1/7)
Four pieces: 33.6 × 27.2 × 19.7;
26.2 × 27.5 × 17.8;
18.5 × 50.5 × 29.2;
13.6 × 44.5 × 34.6
Courtesy of Woltjen/Udell Gallery, Edmonton

34. *Untitled* 1985
Bronze and acrylic paint (artist's proof)
33.6 × 27.2 × 19.7
Collection of Karen Dushinski.
Courtesy of Woltjen/Udell Gallery, Edmonton

35. *Vincent* 1985
Bronze, patina and oil paint (2/7)
99.7 × 68.5 × 19.2
Courtesy of the artist
and Susan Whitney Gallery, Regina

36. *Cézanne I* 1986
Bronze, patina and acrylic paint
54.1 × 29.1 × 42.2
Courtesy of the artist

37. *Cézanne II* 1986
Bronze, patina and acrylic paint
58.1 × 28.3 × 26.8
Courtesy of the artist

38. *Cézanne III* 1986
Bronze, patina and acrylic paint
82.4 × 43.6 × 32.8
Courtesy of the artist

39. *Doug* 1986
Bronze and patina (4/7)
17.9 × 52.9 × 31.4
Collection of the Regina Public Library
Purchased with funds from The Canada
Council Special Purchase Assistance
Programme 1987

40. *Gauguin* 1986
Clay, acrylic paint, wood and wicker
41.3 × 29.1 × 23.2
Courtesy of the artist

41. *The Painter* 1986
Bronze, patina and acrylic paint (7/7)
with wood and arborite base
64.7 × 53.3 × 22.8 (sculpture);
94.0 × 64.0 × 33.0 (base)
Courtesy of the artist

42. *Assyrian Cows* 1987
Bronze and patina
Five pieces, each 29.8 × 50.3 × 5.4
Private collection.
Courtesy of Susan Whitney Gallery,
Regina

43. *Nos Nouveaux Veaux* 1987
Bronze and patina
Six pieces, each 96.5 × 73.0 × 28.2
Courtesy of Woltjen/Udell Gallery, Edmonton

44. *Vincent Self-Portrait Series* 1983-87
Clay and acrylic paint
Forty pieces, average dimensions
25.0 × 17.0 × 6.5
Courtesy of the artist